POPE JOHN XXIII ILLUSTRATED

Alfonso Borello

Pope John XXIII Illustrated - Copyright © 2019 by Alfonso Borello. All Rights Reserved.

All rights reserved. No part of this book may be reproduced in any form or by any electronic or mechanical means including information storage and retrieval systems, without permission in writing from the author. The only exception is by a reviewer, who may quote short excerpts in a review.

Illustrations and cover design by Alfonso Borello

Printed in the United States of America

First Printing: June 2019
Villaggio Publishing Ltd

CONTENTS

Part One 4
Part Two 30
Preview Chapter 46

Alfonso Borello

I've put my eyes in your own eyes, I've put my heart close to yours, and I want to let you know that this encounter with you shall remain forever in my soul.

Pope john xxiii

Part One

I WANTED to lie down in comfort as I explained to the craftsman back when I was experimenting with this box. "Is there anything you can do to make it slightly wider?" I asked.
"Well, in this case I must talk to the master craftsman for a redesign." Replied the artisan.
"I'm a big man, as you can see, but if it is too much of a trouble, I could lie down on the side, I shall fit anyway." The pope explained.
Now that I'm finally at rest, I must tell you that comfortable I am, in a way; there isn't much space to move around, as you shall experience yourself one of these days, but I must accept what it's been offered to me, and so shall you.
I've been out of the scene for quite a while now. Everything is different in here, and the most interesting thing is that you can hear everything,

A young Giuseppe Roncalli, later
Papa Giovanni XXIII.

anywhere at any given time without been seen and judged.
On April 1999 my first and only miracle which dated back to 1962, was actually called miracle, and on September 2000 I was blessed, just a tiny step below sainthood. I'm not boasting, I heard it with my own ears.
Back when someone was still listening to me, I told everybody that I had the good fortune to live in a garden of hope, not in a museum. I told politicians to dust off old ideas from their thrones and focus on what very soon will make us one nation. Back then, I heard the cries of the not so fortunate, the unhappy; sadly, I can still hear their laments.
For the records, I was born poor in a small country village in the Kingdom of Italy; on a rainy Sunday afternoon I was registered as citizen no. 1,200. At age ten I said goodbye to my family and went to school. I was a terrible student, but I loved history. At age twenty-one I joined the army, not by choice. A year later I was able to finish my studies and went back to my home town where I was appointed President of the Society of the Propagation of Faith. Back then people worked in factories eleven hours a day; and after a few days at my new job I witnessed one

The oecumenical council of Pope John XXIII after 50 years hiatus.

of the very first strike; the subtext was: we had enough. I remember very well when my boss took side of these poor souls, he proposed a raise and fewer working hours, and he was promptly accused of fomenting modernism. A few years later I was drafted as a reservist back in the army; days after the boot camp, Italy declared war to Austria and Hungary. I saw things I didn't want to see; the hospital where I was assigned didn't have enough beds and had hardly any medicines. Two pills, a red one for headaches and a white one for infections—a military theory. War had only one meaning, slaughter. The political views of the Italians changed quite often during those difficult years, and at the end of World War I nobody had any idea on what was to happen after.

In the summer of 1924, year of elections, I wrote a letter to my family expressing my concern; no, I have no desire to vote for the fascists; Mussolini will never solve Italy's problems.

The year was 1929 when a treaty between the Vatican and the state of Italy was signed. It was no doubt a treaty of convenience, perhaps of respect; I'll leave you alone if you leave me alone. I didn't have the good fortune to see the fall of Mussolini, because in 1925 I was transferred to Bulgaria where I've spent ten years as Apostolic Visitor, an ambassador of the Catholic

Church; my complicated task was to convert Orthodox into Christians; it wasn't a walk in the park, I guarantee you. During my sojourn in Bulgaria I was in the middle of a crisis when Boris III, Tsar of Bulgaria married Giovanna, daughter of Vittorio Emanuele III king of Italy; the ceremony was first held in Assisi, according to Catholic traditions, but was later celebrated again in an Orthodox church in Sofia; of course, this caused outraged at the clergy, and it became a diplomatic mess.

In 1935 I was in Turkey as Apostolic Delegate; I was later nicknamed Diado, the good father; the country remained neutral during the war and in 1942 in Istanbul, which became the only true Centre for international diplomacy, I had a meeting with Franz von Papen, then German ambassador to Turkey; my humble attempt was to persuade Germany and England to orchestrate a peace treaty, but it failed miserably when Churchill jerked his cane up in the air and blatantly remarked: no treaty with Hitler. After my brief stint as Apostolic Nuncio to France and the agonizing end of World War II, I was summoned to Nuremberg War Crimes Trial where Papen was one of the defendants; I made clear that he gave me the opportunity to save over 24,000 Jewish lives, and the court acquitted him.

Always escorted with joy.

In 1953 I was appointed Patriarch of Venice by Pius XII; the Sunday gondola parades were numerous, theatrical, and tiring, but one of the best day of my life came when I was invited to France at the Elysee Palace to receive my red hat by President Auriol as sign of esteem.

In 1958 the staunch opponent of the Italian Communist Party, the silent soul on the fate of the Jews, the aristocrat, the eliminator of the Italian majority in the College of Cardinals, and later the Righteous Among the Nations at the Yad Vashem Holocaust Memorial, Venerable Pius XII born Giovanni Pacelli, was no longer breathing. Days later, during the conclave I had to face stiff competition between the numerous Cardinals, twenty-four were older than I, and the Italian paper published thirty biographies of potential candidates; the race was wide open. Giuseppe Siri, Genoa Emeritus was the youngest, he was only fifty-two, and the joke was that if he would have been elected, the church would no longer have a Holy Father, but an eternal one. On October 28 at four in the afternoon:

Habemus Papam; I announce to you with great joy: We have a Pope. The most eminent, the most reverend Lord. Lord Angelo Giuseppe Cardinal of the Holy Roman Church Roncalli, who takes the name of John XXIII.

And here I gave my Urbis et Orbis blessing.

So, how do you become a man of love, beyond religion, beyond culture, beyond nation? Just by saying so. Some criticized me for withholding the message revealed in 1917 by the Virgin Mary's apparition at Fatima which was supposed to be made public in 1960. Was it really a message? What so terrible was soon going to happen?

Over the last two centuries it's been said that the mother of Jesus has appeared frequently giving some visionaries plenty of messages. She prophesied a terrible fate to all men who refused to end degeneration and corruption, and she announced the justice of the heavenly Father and the return of her son Jesus Christ.

Apparently, a hostile force opposed her request and someone is preventing her messages to be spread to mankind. I'm not done yet. Through these messages, she explains in a modern way the Revelation Book, she announces the punishment of the Kingdom of God on earth after the second coming of her son Jesus Christ. But apparently, she's magnanimous enough to give mankind the option to change its horrible fate of punishment, of pain, provided he repents and returns to spiritual values. Powerful forces are still opposing the universal spreading of her messages, thus not giving men the opportunity to repent.

Back to the office for more work.

Apparently, her desperate pleas have been ignored by humanity which keeps opting for the most rampant materialism, thus committing atrocious crimes. The damage has been done and, according to her, Satan dominates the world. The evil, the Antichrist is now ruling. The Catholic Church, my Church, is failing. We aren't taking care of souls any more, we're preventing the words of the Holy Virgin to reach the faithful with clarity, seriously, and with importance. Yes, we are. The Vatican is now seriously in trouble. The third secret of Fatima is, without doubt, the most striking example. Why?

Let's go back in time, on September 1846, in a small village located in the French Alps, La Salette, near Grenoble, two shepherds had met by chance the day before on the pastures of mount Planeu; it was a Saturday afternoon, they walked their animals to graze over the torrent Sesia when suddenly a globe of light like the sun appeared. With caution, the two approached the sphere in which, of course, appeared a beautiful lady. The Lady. She was sitting; her hands were over her face, her elbows were resting on her knees; her look was very sad, but she stood up and looked at the two shepherds and said: Come my children, don't be afraid, I won't harm you; I have great

An oceanic crowd attends the Sunday message.

words for you. I want you to know that I've been suffering for you for such a long time.

At the end of her message she told them not to reveal the secret until 1858. The message wasn't published at the due date because Napoleon III was at the time at the peak of his power, and such secret was too ambiguous and a potential scandal had to be avoided. Truth is, such message was never revealed in France. In 1879, the booklet with the secret was finally published in Sicily, with the title *The Appearance of The Holy Mother by the mountain of La Salette.*

Here some of the words: What I'm going to tell you shall not remain secret for long; the priests and ministers of my son have become cesspools of impurity and they're crucifying my son once again. The Catholic Church shall experience an undeniable crisis; woe to the inhabitants of the earth, woe to the princes of the Church who are busy piling riches upon riches, who are busy safeguarding their authority and dominating with pride anything around them. We shall only experience hatred, jealousy and lying without love for anything.

Church scandals will soon make headlines, priests will rape boys, sisters will abuse sisters. Men will kill themselves, there will be massacres even in their own houses.

Children with their dolls wait for the pope.

The anti-religious and the anti-clerical governments will come, all at the service of evil values. Who will suffer? Who will beg for mercy and forgiveness? Who will ask the Lady for help and intercession? Someone will command his angels to sentence his enemies to death. I'm not done yet. The prophecy shall also reveal that a new political order will replace the bigots and will bring prosperity and spiritual values. Seasons will be changed and the earth will no longer produce edible fruits, the stars will change orbit, and the moon will reflect feeble reddish light. Rome will lose the faith and shall become the reign of the Antichrist. When will the Lady summon her faithful and the imitators of Christ? It is the end, yes, you shall experience the end of the ends. Pagan Rome will disappear.

To make things worse was Bernadette, she came from a poor family, she was the first of six children, she had asthma, and she always carried the rosary with her. On February 11, 1858 she was with her sister Mary and another friend when they went to collect firewood by the banks of the Gave river; Bernadette was left alone for a while, because she couldn't cross the river; she heard the sound of rushing wind and suddenly, by a small cave, she saw a globe of light in which the Lady made her appearance.

Regina Coeli: an inmate is blessed.

She smiled at her and said: I can't promise to make you happy in this cruel world but I can take you with me to a better place if you agree; will you come for a few days?
Who are you? Bernadette asked.
I am the Immaculate.
After the end of the two weeks Bernadette asked the same question again.
The Lady smiled and said again, I am the Immaculate Conception.
The dogma was proclaimed by Pope Pius IX; the Lady was in fact the Blessed Virgin. After that appearance Bernadette made numerous attempts to return to the cave for clarifications, or just a sense of responsibility, but she was turned down by the local authorities who erected a fence to keep away the crowd, and after that, Bernadette disappeared from public eyes.
So, what was really the message? Is this Lady who makes impromptu appearances an agitator of some sort? Is the Vatican coming to an end? Is the Church of Christ moving to an undisclosed location outside Rome, perhaps even outside Italy? And why a state is inside another state?
The reason the Vatican is such a mysterious place is that some infidels believe we're hiding something.

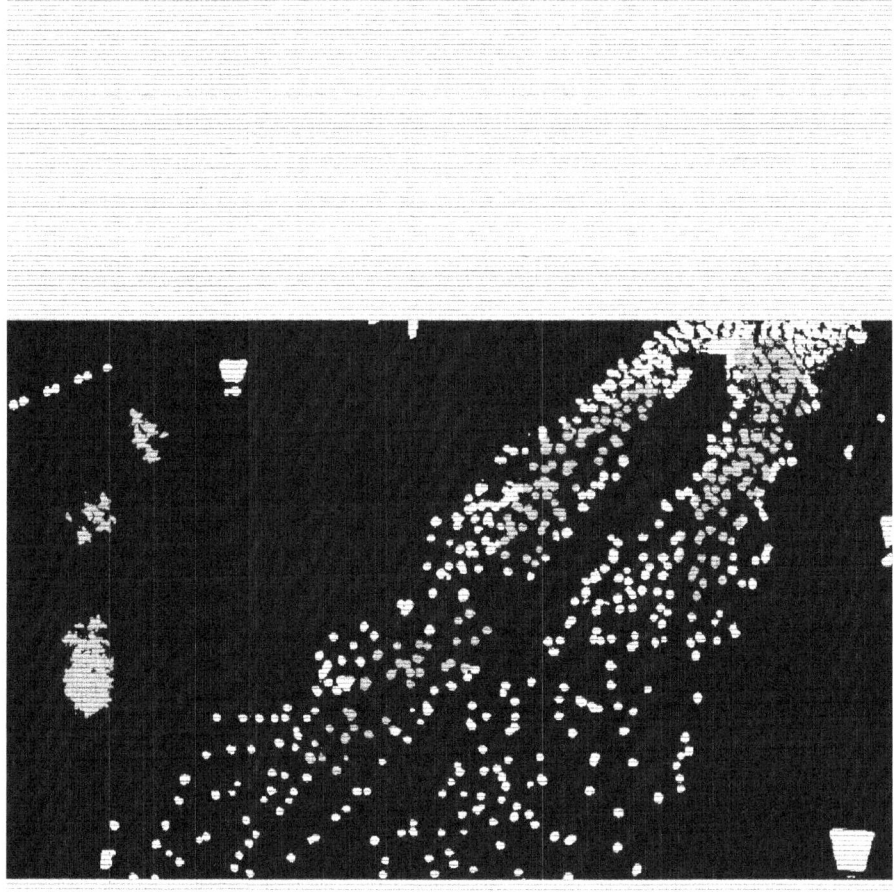

Who are these secret societies people are talking about? Unscrupulous writers fomenting disorders? Illuminati, Freemasons, Templars, and other bogeymen, do they really exist? Did they really kill my predecessor Pius XII and perhaps even Bruce Lee and Michael Jackson?

According to some well-informed individuals, someone is seriously interested in brainwashing the masses and make them believe anything. A new world Order. And more paranoid souls on the other front. It's quite sad, and as well intriguing that history gets rewritten over and over again; some documents disappear, while new ones come out of nowhere with fascinating revelations and of course interpretations. It's also interesting that history books of other countries differ substantially. Who's telling the truth, and, does it really matter?

Was Galileo such a bad guy, the scientist who needed to know everything and create conflicts with our dogmas? Are these charlatans still meeting by the Bernini's masterpiece, The Ecstasy of St. Theresa? What's the secret path, and what's the metaphor in it?

As you're well aware, the Vatican is visited by over thirty million souls every year, and it's somehow challenging to keep track of everyone who mingles and concocts new historical drama around here.

He was the very first pope to use television, the new mass media, to spread his message.

Once upon a time the Roman Church was the only government; it told kings what to do, it financed monarchies, it made laws, it was the only game in town. What's our game now? What's up with the embassy in Washington built in the late eighties? The last and most fascinating theory is that inside the catacombs underneath the Vatican, we're keeping the ashes of St. Peter, and of course Jesus Christ, perhaps even against his will, according to the Church of England. The reason they're both here is because St. Peter was the very first one to see Christ's resurrection, he wasn't but he was instructed to build his own place and apparently, they didn't get along well after completion, and after my extensive walks at night I couldn't find neither.

Money, yes you heard that right. We have plenty of money, we have plenty of gold, and, and... what are the consequences? Why so many popes ended up dead? Power. Secret societies again, or, God forgives me, some other conspiracy?

We had an intruder not too long ago who made a humble attempt to take possession of important documents from the Vatican's archives, papers about the Church involvement in the holocaust and numerous writings by Galileo and Copernicus; he had a long walk inside, because our library is fifty miles

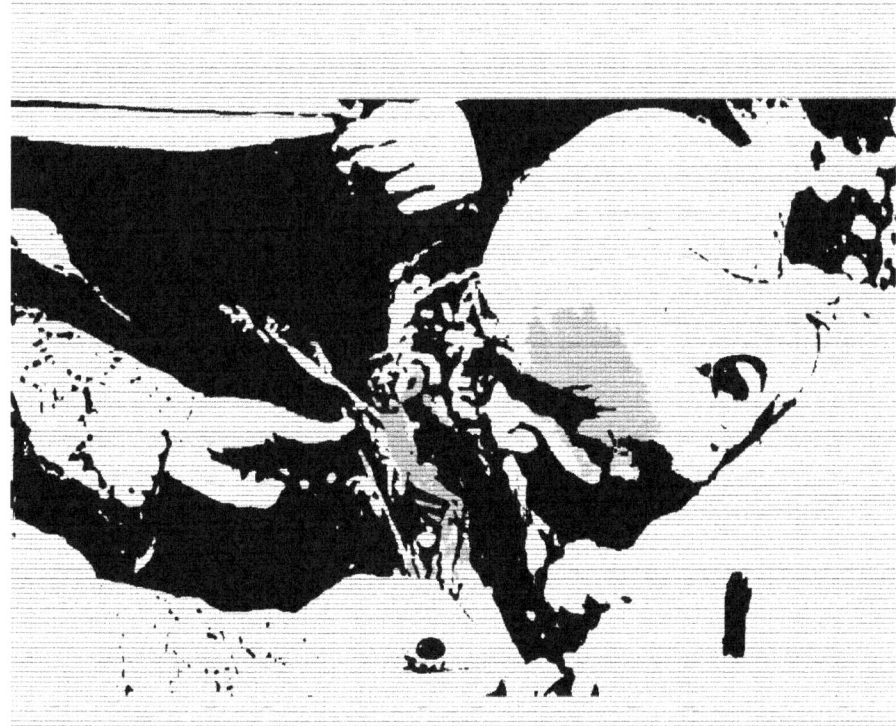

Kneeling to kiss Jesus on Easter Sunday.

long. Another Illuminati's special?

As you can well imagine, being a pope is a tough job, Sunday messages, diplomatic ties, investments, keeping track of priests with hidden life instincts, gathering intelligence on secret societies, and staying alive.

Visiting toddlers at Bambino Gesù Hospital; some children are severly hill.

Part Two

IT'S PAEDIATRIC hospital visit today; not a good place for children, the suffering in here is tenfold and I can't let these unfortunate angels down. I'm dressed in red, I'm short and stocky, and I have plenty of toys in my hands and the children are happy to see me, long live the pope, long live the pope, viva il Papa! They chanted. One tiny soul who kept a severe look on her face since my entrance suddenly stood up and chanted Viva Babbo Natale, long live Santa Klaus; she was instructed to keep quite but her enthusiasm burst into a crescendo; no worries, I said, she's right, I have toys, I'm in red and fat, I only need a hat.

Few days later I went to another house almost forgotten by God, Rome's Regina Coeli penitentiary; such place hadn't been visited by a pontiff in eighty-eight years. I was advised against such visit, but I wanted to let these people know that God had nothing against them, besides they also had loved ones to be blessed, because they were still making an effort to love them. My entrance to this house of penance was ceremonial, it was staged as such, unfortunately the

Inmates around him at Roma's Regina Coeli. No pope has visited the penitentiary in 80 years.

welcome was far from theatrical, it was terribly sterile, and suspicious.

Who's this fat guy and what does he want from us?

My sons and brothers, I said; we're here in the house of the Lord; I know you want to hear a little bit more about me, and here I tell you how I remember when I was a child, and one relative of mine went hunting without a license, he was then arrested and incarcerated right here for an entire month. It was a terrible experience for me to see the Police for the very first time, and it gave me great discomfort to see a man handcuffed. To me it was a cruel initiation to life and its hidden traps. Of course, laws are made for a reason, and sometimes unknowingly you act, but you must later submit to explain your wrongdoing. Well, here I am, now you have seen the Pope, I've put my eyes in your own eyes, I've put my heart close to yours, and I want to let you know that this encounter with you shall remain forever in my soul. Here, at the beginning of the New Year, I shall extend to you my blessing in the name of the Holy Father, and that shall serve as an encouragement for all of you. I want you to write a letter to your family and mention that the pope came here to visit you, but his visit and blessing was also for them, for your wives, and for your children.

An inmate kneels to reach the pope's hand.

According to most, this wasn't the house of the Holy Father, it was the house of men touched by evil; I couldn't let anyone down; I was trembling on my feet, I had knots in my stomach, I had the feeling I was about to fail, and such speech, I must admit, was actually improvised, but it was the very first time in my life as a pontiff that I felt like a real messenger; the end finally turned out to be exquisitely theatrical, and of course I had to leave with some tears, because my dream was much bigger, because I wanted to make a much bigger promise, because I wanted to explain the true meaning of life, but I just did what I could, God forgives me if I failed on that side. My exit was a true ceremony, I felt thousands of hopeful eyes on me, one young man stopped in front of me, he had chains on his feet and almost stumbled, security couldn't do anything to stop him, he knelt down and asked: did you mean the same for me? I embraced him, I didn't say a word, there are times when silence can speak for itself. On October 1962 a snag soon became a real problem when the Soviets and the Americans decided to give a real boost to television viewing; Khrushchev secretly shipped nuclear ballistic missiles to gain military advantage right in America's backyard, Cuba. The CIA took reconnaissance photos of the Soviet build up in the island and promptly informed President John F.

Inside the basilica for the oecumenical council.

Kennedy of the imminent threat. The American President was in the middle of a nightmare and promptly summoned his advisers to discuss the course of action. Three options were outlined: first, accepting the presence and do nothing about it; second, launching air strikes and an amphibious invasion to Cuba; third, create a blockade with the navy. WWIII was the last thing Kennedy had in mind, so he was advised for the third option. If the Soviets will refuse the blockade, they shall be responsible for the consequences, he said. This is a navy job, he continued. Admiral George Anderson was in charge of the mission and replied, Mr. President, the navy will get the job done. The following day American papers ran the headline: 'Highest National Urgency,' Kennedy talks to the nation tonight. The headlines echoed all over the globe, and the beginning of another slaughter, a devastating one considering the technological advances made in those years, seemed very close indeed, of course the motive was a showdown for nuclear supremacy. The small office handling public affairs at the Vatican made substantial efforts to gather intelligence on the Soviet plan; apparently a foxtrot submarine commander by the name of Nikolai Shumkov was ordered to test to ultimate weapon a nuclear torpedo engineered not to hit a single vessel,

A brief cordial meeting with the cardinals.

but to eliminate an entire fleet. Tests were conducted in an area known as the black arbour in the Russian sea with disastrous consequences just a year before, nonetheless Shumkov and other three commanders were ordered to sail for their destination with their diesel powered foxtrots loaded with nuclear torpedoes, and open the envelops with the orders only after reaching the coral bay, only at that point would they learn that they were heading to Cuba, and had the independent authority to fire their weapons without approval from Moscow. It was the first time ever that Soviet submarines were sent on such a long-distance mission in unfriendly waters, and they were given only three weeks to get there; they were ordered to do so in complete secrecy. The stretch between Newfoundland and the Azores was the US navy barrier were all activities from secret submarines were monitored, but a really bad storm with waters at force nine and sometimes ten, gave an edge to the Soviets and the foxtrots were able to slip through. The very first nuclear war was just hours away. Meanwhile American spy planes were flown over Cuba with their camera on, seven missile trailers detected, thirty-six anti-ballistic mid-range missiles, and two long range S-5, tiny mosquitoes of two hundred kilotons with five times the destructive power of the Hiroshima bomb; the film was immediately rushed to the national photographic interpretation centre in Washington. The analysis came out loud and painful, thirteen hundred-mile range missiles capable of killing eighty million Americans

within minutes, all operational in less than a week.

"This government has become aware of the Soviet build up in the island of Cuba. All ships of any kind bound to the island from whatever nation or port, whether carrying cargo or offensive weapons must turn back, and shall be the policy of this nation to regard any missile launched from Cuba into the western hemisphere as an attack by the Soviet Union on the United States; I call upon chairman Khrushchev to halt this clandestine, reckless, and provocative threat to world peace and a stable relation between our two nations, thank you and good night", Kennedy addressed to the American people.

The submarines and the US Navy reached the blockade line at the same time, but the soviet submarines suddenly had a serious problem, they couldn't establish outgoing communication with Moscow because the lines were jammed. Apparently, they could only receive and when they reached the coral barrier, they were instructed to carry onto Cuba and break through by any mean. On the other side Mr. Kennedy began having second thoughts of the effectiveness of the blockade, and contemplated an invasion of the island. In the meantime, two Soviet cargo ships carrying war arsenal were only a few hours away and the Navy mistakenly assumed that the nuclear

A painting of the very first oecumenical council.

submarines were escorting the vessels. They came to the decision to surround the subs and ordered them to surface; the plan was to send a signal with depth charges (flares) without damaging the subs, but there was a problem, any explosion could have been interpreted as an attack. Mr. Kennedy was in the middle of a nightmare—he decided to wait.

The world was waiting and the worst showdown of nuclear supremacy in history was watched by millions on television.

After my noon snack, which consisted of two bread sticks, my secretary read the message which was sent to me directly from President Kennedy. I threw the last bread stick in the rubbish and ordered the drafting of my message with copies going to both American and Soviet embassies. Such was the message:

We beg all governments not to remain deaf to this cry of humanity. That they do all that is in their power to save peace. They will thus spare the world from the horrors of a war whose terrifying consequences no one can predict. That they continue discussions, as this loyal and open behavior has great value as a witness of everyone's conscience and before history. Promoting, favoring, accepting conversations, at all levels and in any time, is a rule of wisdom and prudence which attracts the blessings of heaven and earth.

The following day the message made headlines all over the world, including The Pravda, which ran the headline:

Alfonso Borello

The Sunday ritual: always sold out at St. Peter.

"We beg all governments not to remain deaf to this cry of humanity."

The message had only one thing in mind, give Khrushchev the opportunity to be venerated as a man of peace, and in no way a coward. It worked.

After ten days of tension all Soviet ships reversed course and headed home before reaching the stronghold, and secretly, President Kennedy withdrew American missiles from Turkey.

What really saved the day were four factors, communication problems, fear of the unknown, the triumph of restrain, and a plea for humanity. On July 25, 1963, a month after my death, the US and the Soviet Union signed a nuclear test ban. Who said that being a Pope is just a walk in the garden of the Vatican?

On the train at Rome's stazione Temini.

A special banner: The good pope.

Alfonso Borello

Preview Chapter

THE FORGOTTEN GENIUS, NIKOLA TESLA

A very short biography

Copyright © 2013 by Alfonso Borello
All rights reserved
Published in the United States

SAMPLE

HE TURNED NIGHT into day with the invention of alternate current which is still the standard today; he was the father of over one hundred patents, his genius was shadowed by malefic individuals who called him an eccentric mad scientist, he was ripped off by Thomas Edison for fifty thousand dollars, and the FBI had a large dossier of him which later disappeared. In 1943 he was found dead in a small hotel room in New York. His name was Nikola Tesla. People believed he was out to destroy the world, in reality he was only after progress.

Our success and our failures can't be separated, much like energy and mass, if they would, man would die, he wrote.

In 1891 he patented something truly revolutionary; a small coil would turn 120 volts into 500,000 volts. Let's imagine the flow of electricity through a wire much like water running inside a hose; the voltage can be compared like the pressure of water, if we put a nozzle at the end of the hose, the pressure is substantially increased while the flow diminishes; his coil works on the same principle; the low voltage current goes initially through a spiral and then runs onto another one much longer, which pretty much like a nozzle, reduces the voltage. Now, with the use of a large coil, Mr. Tesla said that he could send an enormous amount of electricity through the earth; we could simply imagine our earth to become a gigantic receptacle. In 1893, Mr. Tesla left New York and moved to Colorado to experiment and prove his theory. His idea was to find the right frequency, big enough and precise enough to pound the earth like it had been hit by a giant hammer.

He built his study center with a 25-meter tower, and the core engine was, of course, this large coil installed at the very top. The local residents witnessed his eccentric experiments and were outraged; according to their credo, Mr. Tesla was an agitator and concocting acts against God.

His experiment was a success, and the large coil was able to output 12 million volts; he was thus able to prove that electricity could be transferred without wires. It was the beginning of something extraordinary.

END OF SAMPLE

About the author

Multiple genres author Alfonso Borello has written drama, thrillers, travel diaries, biographies and essays on history, religion, philosophy, psychology, evolution, cosmos, revolutionaries, inventors, and numerous books in foreign languages and on language learning in Italian, Spanish, Chinese, Tagalog, Cebuano and Thai. Other works include children books, illustrated series, and the Italian Reader application.

Printed in Great Britain
by Amazon